P9-DHF-506

THE ARABIC ALPHABET

THE ARABIC ALPHABET

HOW TO READ AND WRITE IT

BY *NICHOLAS AWDE AND PUTROS SAMANO*

LYLE STUART
Kensington Publishing Corp.
www.kensingtonbooks.com

LYLE STUART books are published by

Kensington Publishing Corp.
850 Third Avenue
New York, NY 10022

Copyright © 1986 Nicholas Awde and Putros Samano

All rights reserved. No part of this book may be reproduced in any form or by any means without the prior written consent of the publisher, excepting brief quotes used in reviews.

All Kensington titles, imprints, and distributed lines are available at special quantity discounts for bulk purchases for sales promotions, premiums, fund raising, educational, or institutional use. Special book excerpts or customized printings can also be created to fit specific needs. For details, write or phone the office of the Kensington special sales manager: Kensington Publishing Corp., 850 Third Avenue, New York, NY 10022, attn: Special Sales Department, phone 1-800-221-2647.

Kensington and the K logo Reg. U.S. Pat. & TM Office
Lyle Stuart is a trademark of Kensington Publishing Corp.

First printing 1987

28   27   26   25   24   23   22   21   20

Printed in the United States of America

ISBN 0–8184–0430–2

Library of Congress Cataloging-in-Publication Data

Awde, Nicholas.
   The Arabic alphabet.
   1. Arabic language—Alphabet. I. Samano, Putros.
   II. Title.
PJ6321.A93   1987   492´.711   86-30042

The Arabic handwriting in this book was done by
Putros Samano.

The authors would like to acknowledge the important assistance
of Jon Rothschild in the preparation of this book.

CONTENTS

A WORD TO THE READER

One of the first obstacles facing anyone trying to learn Arabic is the seemingly complicated and convoluted alphabet, usually treated sketchily in the opening pages of daunting grammatical tomes.

Many students beginning to learn Arabic are plunged directly into grammar lessons without having first mastered the alphabet. They then try to pick the alphabet up as they go, finding out, only too late, that the attempt to assimilate both grammar and the alphabet simultaneously is simply too taxing. Genuine mastery of the alphabet ought to be a *prerequisite* to learning Arabic, yet there is scarcely any material devoted exclusively to it.

But committed students of the language are not the only people interested in the Arabic alphabet. Many others who come into contact with the Arab world would like to be able at least to read a menu or a street sign, to understand labels in a supermarket, or to pay their Arab hosts the simple courtesy of being able to read and write the names of their countries.

This book is meant to suit both the serious student of Arabic and more casual readers: businessmen or tourists visiting the Middle East, employees of British or American companies working for a time in an Arab country, or any of the growing number of people fascinated by the language and culture of a great and increasingly prominent civilization.

The style of the book is light and non-technical: no previous knowledge of grammar or linguistics is assumed. At the same time, we have tried to be meticulous in detail and comprehensive in scope. We have not concealed anything to 'simplify' matters: everything you need to know is here. But neither have we added any unnecessary complications.

The book teaches the alphabet: the letters, sounds, and

writing system of the Arabic language. If you put your mind to it, you will soon find yourself able to recognize and reproduce all the letters, to pronounce them more or less correctly, and to combine them into words. At this point some of you will have reached your goal; others will have taken the first essential step toward mastering Arabic.

How to Use This Book

The first chapter is a brief introduction to the Arabic language. It is intended to give readers the minimum of information required to set a proper context for the presentation of the alphabet. But — and this may seem paradoxical — it actually says more about the basic structure of Arabic than is found in the opening lessons of most university courses.

There are two reasons for this. To start with, learning Arabic is in many ways quite different from learning a European language. If you embark on a study of French, Italian, German — or even one of the more difficult European languages, like Russian or Greek — you soon find that however different from English it might be, there is a basic correspondence in the way the language works overall. In fact, this underlying similarity is so obvious that it is rarely remarked upon, and the beginner feels no sense of disorientation.

In Arabic this is not the case. It is not just that the alphabet and words are unusual. More profoundly, the whole structure of the language — its logical basis so to speak — is alien to the structure of any European language. Even the simplest things — like the distinction between nouns and adjectives — cannot be taken for granted. It is therefore much better (and in the end it makes things easier) if the person embarking on learning Arabic is informed of these structural differences right from the start. A relatively small amount of information can help to reduce that sense of strangeness which all too often overwhelms the European who wants to learn Arabic.

The second reason is simpler: even if all you want to do is learn the alphabet, your task will be facilitated by knowing something about the language that this alphabet expresses. Why, for example, is Arabic usually written without vowels? The answer has to do with the underlying logic of the language.

The chapter introducing the Arabic language is followed by a brief but fairly complete presentation of the whole alphabet and writing system. A table of the main shapes of all the letters is given and their pronunciation discussed. All the various diacritical marks are explained. It is a good idea to read through this brief chapter in one sitting. Don't worry if you don't retain all the information right away. Everything in it is repeated later on, in the main part of the book, which presents all the letters one at a time. After you have worked through these descriptions, you will find that points that may have seemed complicated when you first read chapter 2 now seem easy.

So read through the first two chapters relatively quickly. Try to get the general idea of what is being presented in the second chapter (and concentrate on the information about pronunciation); then keep referring back to chapter 2 as you go through the rest of the book.

When you finish the section explaining each letter, you will be able to move on to reading some simple phrases and sentences. We will then take you, line by line, through the opening sura (or chapter) of the Koran, as a famous sample of Arabic prose. The map at the back of the book gives the names of all the countries and capital cities of the Middle East and North Africa in Arabic.

A last word of advice. Although the Arabic script looks complicated and forbidding at first glance, it is actually quite logical and well-adapted to the Arabic language. It is based on the same principles as the Roman alphabet and is therefore within the reach of anyone who wants to make the effort to master it. Most of all it takes practice. Don't be put off by fear of the unknown. It is not as hard as it looks.

1 INTRODUCTION TO ARABIC

Arabic is one of the world's major languages. It is widely spoken on two continents, across the entire breadth of North Africa to the Arabian peninsula and the entire Middle East. It is the official language of eighteen countries with a total population of about 120 million,* placing it among the top ten tongues of the planet in number of speakers.

Its unbroken literary tradition goes back about thirteen centuries, it is the language of one of the world's major religions — Islam — and it is the written and spoken means of communication in a region of steadily rising importance in international affairs: the Middle East. The numerical, geographical, political, and cultural status of the language was formally recognized by the United Nations in 1973, when Arabic was made the sixth official language of that body (the others are English, French, Spanish, Russian, and Chinese).

Arabic belongs to the Semitic family of languages, which also includes Hebrew (both classical and modern), Aramaic, Syriac, and several of the languages of Ethiopia (Amharic, Tigrinya, Tigre, and others). Its alphabet, with the occasional modification, is used to write other, non-Semitic languages as well, such as Persian, Urdu, and Kurdish. Until about sixty years ago, Turkish was also written with a modified Arabic alphabet, as were several leading African languages, notably Hausa and Swahili.

*These countries are: Morocco, Algeria, Tunisia, Libya, Egypt, Sudan, Lebanon, Syria, Jordan, Iraq, Kuwait, Saudi Arabia, Yemen, South Yemen, Oman, United Arab Emirates, Bahrain, and Qatar. In addition, of course, Arabic is spoken by the Arab population of Israel and the occupied territories, and there are large numbers of Arabic speakers in southern Iran.

13

Arabic is considered a difficult language to learn. One of the problems is that the term 'Arabic' is used to describe three different forms of the same language: classical Arabic, which is the language of the Koran, the holy book of Islam; colloquial, or spoken, Arabic, as used in the daily lives of the people of the Arab countries; and modern standard Arabic, sometimes also called modern literary Arabic.

Colloquial Arabic shows great diversity from region to region and among different layers of the population. Moreover, the various dialects differ quite considerably from the written language in vocabulary and grammar, as well as in syntax.

There is a direct link between classical Arabic and modern standard Arabic, which is the written language of the entire Arab world today. Any newspaper published anywhere in the Arab world, for instance, can be read without the slightest problem anywhere else in the Arab world. Newspapers, magazines, official documents, poetry, all works of non-fiction, and the vast majority of prose literature are all written in modern standard Arabic, which shows virtually no regional variation. Most radio and television broadcasts (especially news programmes and political speeches) are given in a spoken version of the written language. In other words, every Arab who is literate reads modern standard Arabic (the colloquial languages are not written, except occasionally as dialogue in plays and novels), and because of the widening influence of radio and television throughout the Arab world, nearly every Arab, even if illiterate, will understand the spoken version of modern standard Arabic to some extent.

In many ways, modern standard Arabic is quite close to classical Arabic. The Koran, which was first written down about twelve centuries ago, has always been a major grammatical and linguistic authority. The existence of a commonly accepted literary standard has been a powerful unifying force in the written language. One of the results has been that today's Arabic as written in, say, a newspaper or a popular novel is much closer to the language of the Koran than modern Greek, for example, is to classical Greek, not to mention modern and medieval English, French, or German. As compared to classical Arabic, modern standard Arabic is simpler in grammar and syntax, but the greater difference, as you would expect, is in vocabulary.

The alphabet taught in this book is the one used in both classical and modern standard: in Arabic, unlike in English, German, French, or other European languages, there has been no change at all in the alphabet or in spelling in hundreds of years. So learning the alphabet presented in this book is a necessity for learning any kind of written Arabic. Whether you want to read the Koran in its original language, follow the output of modern Arabic literature, or simply read a menu in an Arab restaurant, the first step has to be the same: to learn to read, write, and pronounce the alphabet.

It is not as complicated as it looks. But when first starting out it does help to know something about the overall structure and shape of the Arabic language, because the alphabet, more than most other alphabets in the world, is closely modelled to the language it was devised to represent.

The most important thing to know right from the start is this: like other Semitic languages, Arabic is based on what is normally called a 'consonantal root system'. What this means is that almost every word in the language is ultimately derived from one or another 'root' (usually a verb) that represents a general, and often quite neutral, concept of an action or state of being. Usually this root consists of three letters. By making changes to these letters, the original-root-concept is refined and altered. There are many ways to make these changes: letters are added to the beginning of the root or tacked on at the end; the vowels between the consonants of the root are changed; extra consonants are inserted into the middle of the root; syllables are appended to the end. Each of these changes produces a new word — and a new meaning: meanings seem literally to grow out of the root like branches of a tree. But the original, basic idea of the root persists, in one way or another.

It is easier to see this by taking an example. The three consonants, k, t, and b — combined in that order: k-t-b — connote the idea of writing. The simplest word based on those letters is *kataba*, which means 'to write'. That is the *root*. If you go to an Arabic dictionary and look up the root *kataba*, you will find, among many other entries, the following (the three letters of the root are printed in bold type so that they stand out).

kataba	to write
kattaba	to make someone write
takaataba	to write to each other, correspond
istaktaba	to dictate
kitaab	book
maktab	office
maktaba	library (also bookstore)
kaatib	clerk
miktaab	typewriter
mukaataba	correspondence
mukaatib	correspondent, reporter
muktatib	subscriber
kutubii	bookseller
kutayyib	booklet
maktuub	written (or letter)

The connection of all these words with the underlying idea of writing is pretty clear. But often it is a lot less obvious, more akin to an etymology in an English dictionary: once you read it, you see the connection, but you might not have noticed it on your own. For instance: *katiiba* means 'squadron' or 'military detachment', which seems to have been derived from the time-honoured practice of drawing armies up into battalions on paper before they were actually put into the field.

Now take another look at the list of **k-t-b** words. Apart from the fact that the sequence **k-t-b** appears in every word, you can also notice certain kinds of changes that might easily be seen as patterns that could be repeated with other roots. For example, how do we get *maktab* out of *kataba*? Well, first we *prefix ma-* to the root, and then we delete the first vowel (the *a* after the *k*). Let's take a completely different root and make the same change. Say we have the root **d-r-s**. Its simplest form is *darasa* (just like *kataba*). So let's put in *ma-* as a prefix, take away the *a* after the *d* (and in this case tack on an *-a* at the end, which happens to be just the feminine ending). We get *madrasa*. Now, if we tell you that *darasa* means 'to study', you might not be surprised to find out that *madrasa* means 'school'. A *madrasa* is a place where **d-r-s** takes place (at least in principle), and a *maktab* is a place where **k-t-b** takes place.

Another example. We can get *kaatib* (clerk) from *kataba* (to write) by doubling the first vowel (lengthening it, actually), changing the second vowel from *a* to *i*, and eliminating the final vowel. Now let's take another root, a little more grisly this time: **q-t-l**, or *qatala*, which means 'to kill' or 'to murder'. If we lengthen the first vowel, change the second vowel to *i*, and eliminate the last vowel, we get *qaatil*, which means 'killer' or 'murderer'. Generalizing from these two instances, we might be tempted to say something like this: if we have a three-consonant root and we lengthen the first vowel, change the second vowel to *i*, and eliminate the final vowel, we get a noun that means a person who does the thing that the root word means. A clerk writes and a killer kills. From *kataba* to *kaatib* and from *qatala* to *qaatil*.

Unfortunately, things are not always that simple. In fact, they almost never are. One of the things you can do to a three-consonant root is double the middle consonant (starting with *kataba*, for instance, we get *kattaba*, two *t*'s instead of one). This gives us a new verb. Sometimes that new verb has the connotation of 'making someone do whatever the root word means', as is the case with **k-t-b**, where *kataba* means 'to write' and *kattaba* means 'to make someone write'. But sometimes it can be just an intensified version of the root word. For example, *kasara* (**k-s-r**) means 'to break', while *kassara* means 'to smash'. Moreover, not every three-consonant root uses all its possibilities. There are plenty of sets of three consonants that just never double the middle consonant. For instance, *taraka* (**t-r-k**) means 'to leave', but there is no such word as *tarraka*. It's just a kind of empty form lying there waiting for a meaning to come along and fill it. Sometimes, on the other hand, things can be the other way around: *dallasa* (**d-l-s**) means 'to swindle', also 'to forge' or 'to counterfeit', but there is no such word as *dalasa*. Here the root itself has disappeared, if indeed it ever existed.

The ramifications of a meaning-system like this are virtually endless, and its subtleties are such that you can often quite legitimately end up with words that have a common root but are opposite in meaning. On the other hand, the possibilities of coining new words, of finding an appropriate root and an appropriate 'unfilled form' to correspond to a new idea, are immense. (One example: the modern Arabic word for 'socialism' is *ishtirakiya*, which comes from the root *sharaka*, the *sh* being a single letter, which means 'to share'. Ironically enough, the word for 'corporation', in the sense of 'limited company', is *shirka*, which comes from exactly the same root.)

It should also be remembered that most native speakers of the language do not think about the system in this kind of clinical way, any more than speakers of Romance languages think about how their tongues are related to Latin or any more than English speakers think about the difference between 'strong' and 'weak' verbs. It is an instinctive process in Arabic, as in any language. But for foreigners learning the language it is important to know, right from the beginning, that when they embark on learning Arabic, they are studying a language the key to which lies in its underlying structure of three-consonant roots. Even at the stage of simply learning the alphabet, it helps matters to be aware that the Arabic language is ultimately based on *patterns*. There are many different kinds of patterns, and each may have a variety of possible connotations, but the existence of these patterns is the heart of the language. Even something so elementary as the alphabet is tailored to reflect these patterns.

Because of the emphasis on consonants, it is not surprising that the Arabic alphabet consists almost purely of consonants. In fact, of the twenty-nine letters of the alphabet, twenty-six are consonants, and of the other three, two sometimes stand for consonants as well.

But in certain patterns, those three letters can stand for long vowels. Normally, short vowels are not written. (The *ee* in the English word *reed* is a long vowel; the corresponding short vowel is the *i* in the word *bit*, for example.) Short vowels are not part of the alphabet; when it is considered necessary to write them, they are represented as little hooks and dashes above and below the letters. This means that written Arabic normally looks like a kind of speedwriting: it is as if the words 'modern standard Arabic' were written 'mdrn stndrd rbc'. Now, this is definitely a problem for people learning the language. But the system of patterns makes it less of a problem than it would be in a European language, which would often be completely unintelligible if written without any vowels. Although the lack of vowels may be an obstacle to the learner in the early days, it will rarely cause an Arab to stumble when reading a written unvowelled text; this is because of the patterns.

Once you get used to the various patterns, the lack of short vowels becomes less of a problem. On the other hand, an advantage of Arabic is that the alphabet and writing system is closely tailored to fit Arabic phonetics: if all the short vowels and other diacritical marks are written (as they are, for instance, in all editions of the Koran), then every word is pronounced exactly as it is written and written exactly as it is pronounced.

Another important thing about the writing system: the script is *cursive*. That is, almost all letters are joined up to the letters preceding and following them, as in English longhand. There is no distinction between printing and writing of the sort that exists in European languages: one system in which the letters are joined up and one in which they are kept separate. Also, there are no capital and small letters: the very concept is completely foreign to Arabic. A word that starts a sentence is written just exactly as it would be if it was in the middle of a sentence, and the letter that begins a proper name like Muhammad is exactly the same as that letter when it begins a common word like *maktab*.

But since the letters are almost all joined together (there are just a few that aren't), they take different forms depending on where they appear in a word. For example, when an *m* starts a word, it has to have a little tail connecting it to the next letter of the word. When it comes in the middle of a word it needs two tails, one connecting it to the letter that comes after it and one connecting it to the letter that comes before it. When it is the last letter of a word it needs a tail connecting it to the letter that came before it, but no tail connecting it to the next letter, since there is no next letter; instead it has a special little ending flourish. Finally, when a letter is written by itself, not connected to anything, it usually has a slightly different shape than it would in a word.

At first glance this can seem incredibly complicated: most of the letters have *four* forms each! And most Arabic grammar books start out with a table showing all the various forms laid out in a chart that looks like it was designed to scare off all but the most determined. (We have a table like that too, but at the back of the book, where it belongs — for reference only.) Actually, however, things are not so bad. In general, the *basic shape* of each letter is given by the way that letter looks when it is standing alone in splendid isolation. All the other forms are really only ways to make that basic shape fit into the various combinations with other letters, and once you learn to look at it that way, it soon becomes second nature to you. The best way to learn the alphabet is not to try to memorize a complicated table, but to take each letter one by one, to learn the basic shape first — how to recognize it and how to write it — and then to see how to connect it to other letters. That is what we will do in the pages that follow.

First there will be a list of all the twenty-nine letters of the alphabet. They will be given in their 'isolated' form. Alongside each letter you will find the Arabic name of the letter, the English letters we are using in this book to transliterate the Arabic letters, and a 'guide to pronunciation', which is a rough indication of the sound of each letter. After the table there are a series of notes and explanations about pronunciation and other things you have to know about the writing system. At this stage, just read through them. Then use the table for reference. Later on we will go through each letter one by one, giving all its various forms and showing how all the letters are combined into words.

One last — but very important — point: *Arabic is written from right to left.*

2 THE ALPHABET AND WRITING SYSTEM

The following chart lists the names of all the letters of the Arabic alphabet. The transliteration gives a hint about pronunciation. All letters for which there is no English equivalent are discussed below.

Name of Letter	Arabic Form	Transliteration	Guide to Pronunciation
'alif	ا	aa	fair
baa'	ب	b	big
taa'	ت	t	tell
thaa'	ث	th	think
jiim	ج	j	measure
Haa'	ح	H	no equivalent
khaa'	خ	kh	Scottish loch
daal	د	d	dead
dhaal	ذ	dh	then
raa'	ر	r	rolled r
zaay	ز	z	zoo
siin	س	s	sew
shiin	ش	sh	shall
Saad	ص	S	no equivalent

Daad	ض	D	no equivalent
Taa'	ط	T	no equivalent
DHaa'	ظ	DH	no equivalent
ᶜayn	ع	ᶜ	no equivalent
ghayn	غ	gh	no equivalent
faa'	ف	f	*f*ool
qaaf	ق	q	no equivalent
kaaf	ك	k	*k*itten
laam	ل	l	*l*ove
miim	م	m	*m*ask
nuun	ن	n	*n*ever
haa'	ه	h	*h*appy
waaw	و	w, uu	*w*eld, f*oo*d
yaa'	ي	y, ii	*y*ell, br*ee*ze
hamza	ء	,	no equivalent

If the names of the first two letters — *'alif* and *baa'* — sound like *alpha-bet* it is not just coincidence. The Arabic and Roman (and Greek and Russian) alphabets, no matter how different they may look, all have a common distant ancestor. You can also see a hint of this common descent in the sequence *k, l, m, n,* which occurs in both the Arabic and English alphabets.

22

Notice also that various groups of letters have similar shapes. *Baa'*, *taa'*, and *thaa'*, for instance, are exactly the same except that *baa'* has one dot under the letter, *taa'* has two dots above, and *thaa'* has three dots above. These dots are crucial: they are not extra diacritical marks but are part of the letters themselves.

Hints on Pronunciation

In Arabic, as in any language, proper pronunciation is best learned by imitating a native speaker. What follows here is meant to give only a general idea of how the letters sound. By carefully following the instructions here, you can arrive at a good enough first approximation to serve until you are able to listen to Arabs. We'll take the consonants first and then say something about vowels and combinations of vowels.

Consonants

Except for the ones discussed below, the consonants are pronounced pretty much as they are in English. When you see an Arabic letter in the table transcribed by a normal, lower-case English letter (or a combination of two normal, lower-case letters), you can assume that the Arabic letter is pronounced like its English equivalent (like *b, t, d, sh,* and so on). The ones that need some explanation are as follows.

ء *hamza*. Phonetically, the *hamza* is a 'glottal stop'. It sounds like a little catch in the voice. Although there is no letter representing this sound in English (which is why we represent it in the transliteration by an apostrophe), the sound actually does exist. Say the word 'Noel', not as if it were written 'Nowel', but clearly separating the two syllables: 'No-el'. If you did it properly and forcefully, that little catch in your voice between the two syllables was a perfect *hamza*. The traditional Cockney way of saying 'bottle' (as *bo"le*) also has a *hamza* in it. Another way to try it is to say the syllables 'uh-oh' (as though you're in trouble). You should notice that same little catch in the voice at the beginning of each syllable. In Arabic the glottal stop is a full-fledged consonant and can appear in the strangest places: at the end of a word for example. The main thing is: be careful not to ignore it.

Four Arabic letters — ظ , ط , ض , ص — are known as 'emphatic consonants'. They are represented in the transliteration as capital letters. Although there is no exact equivalent of them in English, they are not all that difficult to pronounce: it just takes a bit of practice. The best way to do it is to start with their 'unemphatic' equivalents. For example, pronounce as *s*, as in English. This is the Arabic letter *siin* (س) . Now try to make the same sound, but as if your mouth was full of cotton wool, so that you have to say *s* with your tongue drawn back. Make the sound more forcefully and shorter in duration than a normal *s*. The back of your tongue should be raised up toward the soft palate, and the sound produced should have a sort of 'dark' quality. This is the letter *Saad* (ص) . There is a similar relationship between the following pairs: د and ض (*daal* and *Daad*), ت and ط (*taa'* and *Taa'*); ذ and ظ (*dhaal* and *DHaa'*). If you listen to native speakers of Arabic, one thing you will notice is that these 'emphatic consonants' give a very distinctive sound to the language. To sum up: the four emphatic consonants, with their 'unemphatic' equivalents, are:

س	*s*	ص	*S*
د	*d*	ض	*D*
ت	*t*	ط	*T*
ذ	*dh*	ظ	*DH*

While we're on the subject, notice that Arabic has two different letters to represent the two sounds of *th* (as in *think* and as in *then*). The second one (*th* as in *then*) is represented in the transliteration as *dh*.

The letter *khaa'* (خ) , represented in transliteration by *kh*, is like the *ch* in the Scottish *loch*, or like the *ch* in the German pronunciation of the composer *Bach*. But it is slightly more guttural than its Scottish or German cousin. Whatever you do, don't pronounce it as an *h* or a *k*. It is better to exaggerate rather than underemphasize the guttural aspect.

24

The letter *ghayn* (غ) is another one that gives English-speaking people trouble. More or less, it is the sound you make when gargling. Everyone can do it, but it's not always easy to get used to it when it appears in words. Another way to approximate it pretty well: it is almost exactly the sound of the very strongly rolled Parisian *r* in French.

Now we come to the three letters that always give European speakers the most trouble.

Qaaf (ق) , represented by *q* in the transliteration, sounds a bit like *k*, but is pronounced very far back in the throat. When you say the letter *k*, you touch the roof of your mouth with more or less the middle of your tongue. When you say a *qaaf*, you touch the very back of your tongue to the soft palate in the back of your mouth. Most Europeans trying to learn Arabic have a lot of trouble doing this, and pronounce *qaaf* as if it were *kaaf*. Arabs tend to be fairly tolerant of this mistake, and there are not very many words in which the difference between *qaaf* and *kaaf* determines a different meaning. Still, it's worth making the effort.

You probably noticed that one of the letters of the Arabic alphabet – ع – is transliterated by a raised letter ᶜ. The reason for this peculiarity is that this letter is completely foreign not only to English but also to any other European language, and in fact to just about all the world's languages. It is a peculiarity of the Semitic languages, and one of the most difficult sounds of the Arabic language to make. Unfortunately, it is also one of the most common letters. The only real way to learn it is to listen to Arabs and to practice incessantly. In scientific phonological terms, this letter is a pharyngal voiced fricative. That means that the sound is made by constricting the muscles of the larynx so that the flow of air through the throat is partially choked off. One eminent Arabist once suggested that the best way to pronounce this letter is to gag. Do it, and you'll feel the muscles of your throat constrict the passage of air in just the right way. The sound is *voiced*, which means that your vocal cords vibrate when making it. It sounds rather like the bleating of a lamb, but smoother.

Finally, we have *Haa'* (ح) , transliterated by a capital *H*. *Haa'* sounds much like a very emphatic *h*. Imagine that you've just swallowed a spoonful of the hottest chili imaginable: the 'haaa' sound that results should be a pretty good approximation of *Haa'*. Strictly speaking, *Haa'* is an unvoiced version of ʿ*ayn*. In other words, it is made just like the ʿ*ayn*, except that when you say ʿ*ayn* your vocal cords vibrate, but when you say *Haa'* they don't. (In English, for instance, *t* and *d* are exactly the same, except that *t* is unvoiced and *d* is voiced: your vocal cords vibrate when you say *d*, but not when you say *t*.)

Don't worry too much if you can't get *qaaf*, ʿ*ayn*, and *Haa'* right away. Quite a few learned people have struggled for decades with them. As a first approximation, you can pronounce *qaaf* like *kaaf*, ʿ*ayn* like *hamza*, and *Haa'* like *haa'* (like an English *h*). But this should be only a temporary measure, more or less equivalent to the Arab who says 'blease' instead of 'please' (as you will have noticed, there is no letter *p* in Arabic). ·

One last point: the letter *raa'* (ر) is always rolled: exaggerate it rather than lose it.

Vowels

Written Arabic has only three vowels — *a*, *u*, and *i*. But they come in pairs: each vowel can be either long or short. The difference between long and short vowels is important in both speech and writing, and the distinction actually affects meaning in many words (*faaris*, for example, means 'Persia', whereas *faras*, with a short *a*, means 'horse').

The short vowels *a*, *u*, and *i* are not part of the main alphabet. Instead they are written as small 'blips' or strokes above or below the consonants that come before them in pronunciation. The short *a* is pronounced like the *a* in the English word *pat*, the short *u* is like the *u* in *put*, and the short *i* is like the *i* in *pin*. The *a* is represented as a slanted slash above the consonant; the *u* is represented by a sort of miniature *waaw* above the consonant;

the *i* is represented by a slash just like the *a* but *below* the consonant. For example, let's take the letter *daal* (which, remember, has the sound *d*); with the three short vowels it would be written

َد *da*

ُد *du*

ِد *di*

The long vowels *aa*, *uu*, and *ii* are represented in writing by the three letters *'alif* (١), *waaw* (و), and *yaa'* (ي) respectively. As we mentioned before, these vowels are actually pronounced *longer* than their short counterparts: it really does take longer to say them, in fact about twice as long as it does to say the short vowels. The *aa* comes out sounding more or less like the *ai* in the English word *fair*, the *uu* like the *oo* in *food*, and the *ii* like the *ee* in *breeze*. It is important to remember, however, that Arabic vowels are all *pure*: in other words, the position of tongue and lips must remain stationary while the vowels are pronounced. This is rarely true in English, where, for example, the word *food* is often pronounced as if it had a half-silent *w* in it. Finally, you will notice in the alphabet table that besides representing the long vowels, the letters *waaw* and *yaa'* also stand for the consonants *w* and *y*. How can you tell when a *waaw* stands for *w* and when it stands for a long *uu*, and when a *yaa'* stands for *y* and when it stands for a long *ii*? The answer is that when one of these letters stands for a consonant it will itself be marked with a short vowel; when it stands for a long vowel, it will have no vowel sign at all on it.

To clarify this, let's take the consonant *daal* again. If *daal* is followed by the three long vowels, it is written

دا *daa*

دُو *duu*

دِي *dii*

Notice that in each case the *daal* is marked with a short vowel as well as the corresponding long vowel after it. On the other hand, if *waaw* and *yaa'* stood for consonants and not long vowels, we would have

$$ \text{دَوَ} \quad dawa $$

$$ \text{دَيِ} \quad dayi $$

Here *waaw* and *yaa'* are themselves marked with short vowels, and therefore must be consonants.

When *no vowel* follows a consonant, a sign called *sukuun* is written over that consonant. The *sukuun* looks like a small zero (°), which is a convenient way of thinking about it: it means zero vowel.

Arabic also has two diphthongs. A diphthong is a combination of two vowels written and spoken together. The first diphthong has more or less the sound of the *ow* in the English word *how*. It is composed of a short *a* followed by *waaw* and is thus transliterated *aw*. The second sounds like the *i* in *bite*. It is composed of a short *a* followed by *yaa'* and is thus transliterated *ay*. A *sukuun* written over a *waaw* or a *yaa'* is the main indication of a diphthong. Using the letter *daal* again:

$$ \text{دَوْ} \quad daw \text{ (sounds like English } dow\text{)} $$

$$ \text{دَيْ} \quad day \text{ (sounds like English } die\text{).} $$

Summarizing all this, we can draw the following chart, which gives the combinations of all six Arabic vowels (three short and three long) and two diphthongs with the letter *daal*.

✓	دَ *da*	اَد *daa*
ﻭ	دُ *du*	دُو *duu*
ﹼ	دِ *di*	دِي *dii*
	دَوْ *daw*	دَيْ *day*

Other Signs

Doubled Letters

Arabic, unlike most European languages, does not bother to write a letter twice in words like *bitter* or *twaddle*. Instead there is a special sign, written above a letter, that means that this letter should be read as if it appeared twice. This sign is ّ and is called *shadda* or *tashdiid*. This is important in pronunciation, because of the patterns that we talked about before. Remember, for instance, that if you double the middle consonant of a three-consonant root, you get a new verb that may mean 'to make someone do' whatever the root word means. The word *darasa* means 'to study', but the word *darrasa* means 'to make someone study', or more precisely, 'to teach'. Now, *darasa* would be written

دَرَسَ

but *darrasa* would be written

دَرَّسَ

The *shadda* makes all the difference. Make sure to pronounce *darrasa* with the two *r*'s clearly distinct: *dar-rasa*. The same with any other doubled consonant.

Hamza

We have already talked a bit about *hamza* (ء), the consonant that is pronounced like a catch in the voice. Although the *hamza* is a full consonant in Arabic just like any other, it is written in a special way. Only very rarely can a *hamza* stand on its own. Most often the *hamza* is written 'riding' on another letter. That letter can be either *alif* (ا), *waaw* (و), or *yaa'* (ي). There is a set of very complicated rules that determine which letter the *hamza* must 'ride on' in any given word — so complicated, in fact, that most Arabs never learn them all. Later on, we will give a simplified form of those rules and we will see how the *hamza* is written in almost every context. For the moment, note just this one point: whenever a *hamza* comes at the beginning of a word, that *hamza* 'rides' on an *'alif*. If the following short vowel is *a* or *u*, the *hamza* will sit on top of the *'alif*; if the following short vowel is *i*, it will sit underneath the *'alif*. Thus:

أُ	'*u*
أَ	'*a*
إِ	'*i*

When you see one of these combinations at the beginning of a word, remember *not to pronounce the 'alif*. In this context, the *'alif* has no value of its own: its only role is to 'carry' the *hamza*.

taa' marbuuTa

Arabic has two genders, masculine and feminine. Many nouns and adjectives are made feminine by adding an ending to the masculine form. The most common feminine ending is the so-called *taa' marbuuTa*, which means 'tied *t*'. The *taa' marbuuTa* is simply the letter *haa'* (ه) with two dots over it: ة. In other words, it is a kind of combination of *h* and *t* (having the shape of *haa'* with the two dots of *taa'*). If a *taa' marbuuTa* is followed by a vowel, it is pronounced as a *t*; otherwise it is pronounced simply as short *a* or as *ah*. For example, the word for 'administration' — *'idaara* — is written thus

$$إِدَارَة$$

and, as indicated in the transliteration, the *taa' marbuuTa* at the end would be pronounced as short *a*. But if the word 'administration' were followed by another word with an intervening vowel, it would be pronounced *'idaarat*, with the *taa' marbuuTa* pronounced as a *t*.

madda

The *madda* is a special symbol to represent a particular sound. Suppose a word started with *hamza* followed by the long vowel *aa*. Since *hamza* at the beginning of a word always 'rides' on an *'alif* and since *'alif* also represents the long vowel *aa*, we would have

$$أَا$$

This is considered ugly and unwieldy, so a special symbol, the *madda*, has been invented to stand for the sound *'aa*. It looks like this:

$$آ$$

Case Endings

Classical Arabic had three cases: nominative, accusative, and genitive. This meant that the ending of a word would change depending on its role in the sentence. (Remnants of cases exist in English too. That's why you say 'she did it' and 'he gave it to her' but not 'her did it' or 'him gave it to she'.) In Arabic these cases were indicated by modified versions of the short vowels added to the end of the words. In addition, each case had two sets of endings, one used for words that were 'defined' (like '*the* book'), another for words that were 'undefined' (like 'book' or '*a* book'). That made a total of six possible endings, two each, defined and undefined, for nominative, accusative, and genitive.

Now, in modern Arabic, both spoken and written, these endings have in practice almost disappeared, just as they have in English. Unfortunately, their disappearance is not total. Theoretically, they still exist. Most Arabic courses spend a lot of time on the case endings. The rules for using them are quite complicated, so much so that even among native speakers of Arabic only a small minority have really mastered them. In fact, unless it is your ambition to become a lawyer pleading cases in an Arab court or a Koranic scholar, you are better off spending as little time as possible bothering about Arabic case endings. They are hardly ever written, since with just one exception they are represented by short vowels, and short vowels are hardly ever written. More to the point, they are hardly ever pronounced either.

Then why bother with them at all? Two reasons. First, in a few instances they persist in both the written and spoken languages. Second, if you pick up a fully vowelled text, an edition of the Koran for instance, you will see them written there. So the best procedure is to learn to *recognize* the case endings, so that you are not thrown off when you come across them. Later on, you will gradually come to learn how to use the ones that are still needed. The *sounds* of these case endings are:

	indefinite	definite
nominative	-un	-u
accusative	-an	-a
genitive	-in	-i

Take an example. The word for house is *daar*. If the word is indefinite ('a house' or just 'house'), then the three cases would give us: *daarun* (nominative), *daran* (accusative), *daarin* (genitive). If the word were defined (for instance, 'Muhammad's house', which in Arabic has to be 'the house of Muhammad'), it would be, in the three cases: *daaru* (nominative), *daara* (accusative), *daari* (genitive). Now let's see how these endings are written in Arabic.

The word by itself is

دَار

And with the endings

دَارٌ	*daarun*	دَارٌ	*daaru*
دَارًا	*daaran*	دَارَ	*daara*
دَارٍ	*daarin*	دَارِ	*daari*

Notice that all the indefinite endings involve a doubling up of the short vowels associated with the ending; this doubling of the vowels is read as if it were short vowel plus *n*. For the definite endings we have simply the appropriate short vowel. But notice something else as well: in the accusative indefinite ending (-*an*), there is not only the doubled-up short vowel, but also an extra 'alif. This 'alif is *written but not pronounced*. Now, since none of the short vowels are normally written, the accusative indefinite ending -*an* is generally speaking the only one you will see written, since the 'alif associated with it is always written (but not pronounced).

Accent and Stress

Accent is just as important in Arabic as in English. In English, it is usually impossible to tell which syllable of a word should be stressed, and English is especially complicated in this, since the stress can fall on virtually *any* syllable, whereas in most languages there are restrictions on where accents are allowed to fall. The best way of getting a sense of the stress patterns of any language, of course, is to listen to native speakers and to build up an intuitive sense of rhythm for the language. This is just as true for Arabic as for any other language. But there are some clear guidelines about Arabic stress.

The first thing to note is that Arabic syllables are divided into two kinds: long and short. A short syllable is simply a single consonant followed by a single short vowel. The word *kataba* for instance, is composed of three short syllables: *ka-ta-ba*. Any syllable that is not short is considered long. There are various ways a syllable can be long: a consonant plus a long vowel; a consonant plus a diphthong; a consonant followed by a short vowel followed by another consonant. For instance, *kitaab* ('book') has two syllables, one short (*ki-*) and one long (*-taab*). Another example: *maktaba* ('bookstore' or 'library') has three syllables. The first one is long (*mak-*), the second short (*-ta-*), the third short (*-ba*). Finally, take *maktuub* ('letter'). It has two long syllables (*mak-*) and (*-tuub*).

Now, the basic rule of Arabic stress is this: the accent falls on the long syllable nearest to the end of the word. If the last syllable is long, then that syllable is stressed: *kitaab*, accent on the last syllable. If the second-to-last syllable of a word is long and the last is short, then the second-to-last syllable is stressed: *'abuuhu* ('his father'), accent on the second-to-last syllable. If there is *no* long syllable in the word (like *kataba*), then the accent is on the third-to-last syllable. This will be the case with the great majority of root words, since these usually take the form of three consonants separated by short vowels (*kataba, darasa, taraka,* and so on — all accented on the first syllable). Last point: the accent is not allowed to fall any further back than the third syllable from the end. So if you have a word of four (or more) short syllables, the stress has to fall on the third syllable from the end. For example: *katabahu* ('he wrote it') has four short syllables; the stress will therefore fall on the third syllable back: *katábahu*.

While we're on the subject of accent, we should note one other thing: in Arabic every syllable, long or short, should be clearly and distinctly pronounced, given its due weight. In this Arabic is like Italian, Spanish, or German, and *not* like English or French. Syllables do not disappear or get slurred just because they are unstressed.

Punctuation

This is a grey area in Arabic. Here are some of the more commonly used items:

> comma   ،
> semicolon   ؛
> colon   :
> full-stop   .
> quotation marks   «   »
> question mark   ؟
> exclamation point   !
> dash   —

Numbers

The numerals in Arabic are written like this

٠	١	٢	٣	٤	٥	٦	٧	٨	٩
0	1	2	3	4	5	6	7	8	9

Be careful not to confuse zero and five. The Arabic five looks a lot like our zero, except it is slightly flattened. The dot in the middle of a line is the Arabic zero. Also be careful of two and three, which are very similar in Arabic. And of course, seven and eight. A memory trick to help you remember which is seven and which is eight: 'seven is open to heaven'.

One peculiar thing about Arabic numerals is that even though the language is written from right to left, the numerals are written from left to right, in the same order as European numerals. For instance:

٢٣	٣٥	١٣٧	٢٣٩	١٩٨٦
23	35	137	239	1986

Finally, the numbers given here are the ones used in the eastern part of the Arab world. In North Africa (particularly the three former French colonies Morocco, Algeria, and Tunisia), European numerals are generally used.

Ligatures

Arabic was developed as a *handwritten* script. As a result, combinations of letters were invented to facilitate the flow of writing. In addition, partly because Islam forbids the representation of the human form, calligraphy has come to play a large part in the Arab visual arts, a process no doubt aided by the intrinsic grace of the alphabet, which lends itself to considerable artistic elaboration.

The special combinations of letters — called ligatures — have given Arab printers headaches for ages. Modern Arabic typewriters (as well as many printing styles) have done away with nearly all of them. But since you will still encounter them, here — just for reference — is a table of the most common ones. We will come to some of them later on. It isn't necessary for you to use them — merely to recognize them when you come across them. After you have gone through the whole book, it might be helpful to come back to this page to compare the various ligatures with the way the same letters would normally be written.

ح + ب =	ﲜ	ﻂ	= ح + ل
ح + ح =	ﴦ	ﻞ	= م + ل
ح + ح =	ﲬ	ﻎ	= ح + ف
ح + ح + ح =	ﳗ	ﻞ	= ح + م + ل
ح + س =	ﺵ	ﻣ	= ح + م
ح + ص =	ﴥ	ﯔ	= م + ي

Well, so much for our introductory survey of the Arabic language and its alphabet. Don't worry if you did not retain all the information given. The next step is to go through the letters one by one. Each letter will be explained in detail, and its various forms demonstrated. Along the way, you will learn how to combine the letters into words, and how to string the words together into sentences.

Here are some hints about how to proceed from here on.

1. Pay attention to which letters and which parts of letters go below the line and which go above the line.

2. Try not to take your pen off the page — make your writing look as fluid as possible. Look upon the writing of a word as the writing of a single, extended letter.

3. Put in all the dots and any other accessory part of the word *after* you have finished writing the whole basic shape of the word. Also, put the dots in from *right to left*.

4. Remember that all the examples showing you how to write words and letters flow *from right to left*.

5. After reading any Arabic in this book, copy it out for yourself.

6. Practise the isolated forms of the letters in particular. As we said before, it is the isolated form that determines the *basic* shape of the letter.

7. It might help to take some tracing paper and lay it over the Arabic words in this book and then trace the words out several times, trying to go faster each time until you get the feel of the *flow* of each word. Then try to do the word by yourself on a separate piece of paper.

Finally, once you have completed the section on making all the letters, it would probably be helpful to refer to the chart on pages 93-94, which lists all the various forms of each letter. It is a kind of check-list of the entire alphabet.

3 THE LETTERS

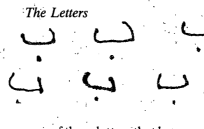

ب (*baa'*) belongs to a group of three letters that have exactly the same shape. The other two are *taa'* (ت) and *thaa'* (ث). These three letters are distinguished only by their dots. These dots are *part of the letters*, and not extra diacritical marks.
ب has one dot below it.

In isolation, it is written like this

Notice that the basic shape is wide and shallow, about three times as long as it is wide. It sits right on the line, and the dot goes just under the line, in the centre of the letter.

ب is one of the letters whose shape changes depending on whether it falls at the beginning, in the middle, or at the end.

The initial form looks like this

The medial form looks like this

The final form looks like this

Notice that the final form is basically the same as the isolated

39

form, except for the little link joining it to the preceding letter. The initial and medial forms too are basically the same thing: a blip in the line with a dot under it. In effect, the isolated and final forms are just the blip of the initial and medial forms with an extra flourish.

A string of forms of the letter *baa'* would look like this

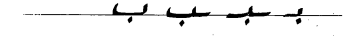

Now, remember that the short vowels (*a, i,* and *u*) are written as small diacritical marks above and below the letters. (Take another look at chapter 2, pp. 26-28, where the short vowels are explained.) We can add these vowels to the letter *baa'* to produce three different syllables, like this

ba	بَ
bi	بِ
bu	بُ

The Arabic names of the short vowels are: *fatHa* (*a*), *kasra* (*i*), and *damma* (*u*).

ت   ث

ت (*taa'*) is exactly the same as *baa'* except that it has two dots above the letter instead of one dot below. The two dots are placed close to each other just above the top of the scoop, so that the letter *taa'*, written in isolation, looks like this

A *taa'* coming at the end of a word would look like this

ﻣﺖ ﺳـﺖ ﻛﺖ ﺳـﺖ

In the initial or medial position, *taa'* is, again, just like *baa'*, except for the dots. Notice that the two dots are placed close together, centred over the blip.

ث (*thaa'*) is just like *baa'* and *taa'*, except this time we have three dots placed over the letter. These dots form a kind of equilateral triangle: the two dots of *taa'*, plus one added on top. The forms therefore look like this

Isolated

ث ﻧﺚ ﻧﺚ ﻧﺎ ﺛ

Final

ﺑﺜﺎ ﺳﺜﺖ ﺳﺚ ﺚ

Initial

ﺛ ﺛـ ﺛـ ﺛـ ﺛـ ﺛـ

Medial

ﺜـ ﺜـ ﺜـ ﺜـ ﺜ

Reminder about pronunciation
The letters *baa'* and *taa'* are pronounced almost exactly like the English letters *b* and *t*. The letter *thaa'* is pronounced just like the *th* in the word *think*.

Remember that on pp. 28-29 we explained the sign called *shadda*, which is how Arabic indicates that a letter is to be pronounced twice. For instance, suppose we wanted to write the sound *tabba*. Instead of writing the letter *baa* twice, we simply write it once and place a *shadda* (ّ) above it, like this

تَبَّ

With this in mind, and with our three letters *baa'*, *taa'*, and *thaa'*, we are now in a position to write some Arabic words. We have picked these words not because of what they mean or because of their frequency, but just to show how these first three letters *can* be combined to make actual words.

بَثْبَثَ	تَبَّ	بَتَّ
bathbatha	*tabba*	*batta*
to spread, scatter	to perish, be destroyed	to achieve, settle

بَثَّ	ثَبَتَ	بَتَّتَ
baththa	*thabata*	*battata*
to broadcast	to be fixed	to cut up

ن

ن *nuun* is very similar to *baa'*, *taa'*, and *thaa'* in two of its forms: the initial and the medial. In fact, the only difference between *nuun* and *baa'* in these two cases is that the single dot goes above the blip instead of below it. So we have

Initial

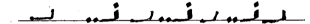

Medial

In the isolated and final forms, however, there is a difference in the shape of the scoop. The same dot is still there, but the scoop of the letter is fuller and more rounded. Also, the scoop of the letter *nuun* drops *below the line*, whereas the scoop of *baa'*, *taa'*, and *thaa'* sits *on* the line.

So for *nuun* we have

Isolated

Final

43

A string of the letter *nuun* would look like this

ن ڻ ـن ـنـ نـ

Reminder about pronunciation
The letter *nuun* is pronounced just like the English letter *n*.

In the beginning, you may find yourself confusing *nuun*, *baa'*, *taa'*, and *thaa'*, especially when they occur in their initial and medial forms, when they are distinguished only by the placement and number of dots. But this is only a matter of practice. In time you will automatically come to associate the sound *b* with a dot below, the sound *n* with a dot above, the sound *t* with two dots above, and the sound *th* with three dots above. As an aid to memory, try this device: *b* below, *t* two, *th* three; *n* you just have to remember.

Here are a few more words combining these letters. Remember from chapter 2 that a little circle over a letter is called *sukuun* and means that the letter in question is followed by *no vowel* ('zero vowel').

تِبْنْ	بِنْت	نَبَتَ
tibn	*bint*	*nabata*
straw	girl	to grow, sprout

بِنْت

بِنْت

ﻱ

ﻱ (*yaa'*) is another letter that has some features in common with the other letters we have considered so far. Its initial and medial forms are the same as all the others, except this time the letter has *two* dots below. The two dots are written close together, and are centred under the blip of the letter. Like this

Initial

Medial

The shape of *yaa'* in its final and isolated forms, however, is quite different from anything that we have had so far. In fact, since your pen has to change direction several times, this is not an easy shape to make, and it requires quite a lot of practice. Follow the direction of the arrows carefully.

Isolated

Final

Reminder about pronunciation
The letter *yaa'* is one of the two letters of the Arabic alphabet

that can stand for a consonant or for a long vowel. It also appears in one of the two diphthongs (vowel combinations).

As a consonant, *yaa'* is pronounced just like the *y* in the English word *yes*.

As a long vowel, *yaa'* represents the sound of *ee* in the word *feet*.

As a diphthong, *yaa'* has the sound of *ei* in the word *neighbour*.

How can you tell, in any given word, whether the *yaa'* is meant to be a consonant (*y*), a long vowel (*ee*), or part of a diphthong (*ei*)? The rule is actually simpler than it may sound. If *yaa'* is itself marked with a vowel, then it is a consonant. If *yaa'* is not marked with a vowel but comes after a consonant that is marked with a short vowel *i*, then it is a long vowel. If *yaa'* is marked with a *sukuun* ('zero vowel') and the letter that comes before it is marked with a short vowel *a*, then it is a diphthong. Look at the following list of five words, and pay careful attention to the transliteration.

يَنْبُت	تِين	بَيْنَ
yanbut	*tiin*	*bayna*
it grows	figs	between

بَيْت	نَبِيّ
bayt	*nabiiy*
house	prophet

In the first word (reading from right to left, of course), the *yaa'*, which begins the word, is marked with a short vowel *a*. It is therefore a consonant, with the sound *y*. In the second word, the *yaa'* in the middle of the word has no vowel, but the *taa'* that comes before it has a short vowel *i*. The role of the *yaa'* in this word is therefore to *lengthen* the vowel, and it has the sound *ee*. In the third and fourth words, the *yaa'*, again coming in the middle of the word, is marked with *sukuun*, the 'zero vowel'. But the first letter of the words (*baa'*) has the short vowel *a*. In these words, then, the *yaa'* is part of a diphthong and has the sound of *ei* in *neighbour*. Finally, look at the fifth word. Here we have a *yaa'* at the end of a word, marked with a *shadda*, which means that the letter is *doubled*. In effect, the first *yaa'* is lengthening the vowel under the *baa'* and the second *yaa'*, which has no vowel, is a consonant. So the word is pronounced with a long *ee* and a *y* at the end.

All this may seem very complex at first, but in time, with practice, it becomes second nature.

Finally, there is one more point we have to make about *yaa'*. A *yaa'* written *without any dots* is sometimes used to represent the sound of the long vowel *aa*. This job is usually done by a different letter, *'alif*, which is the next letter we will deal with. But in some cases — and this happens *only* at the end of a word — a *yaa'* without dots is used instead of *'alif*. In Arabic grammar the *yaa'* without dots at the end of a word is called *'alif maqsuura*. Literally, this means 'shortened *'alif* ', and is so called because the sound *aa*, normally a long vowel, is then pronounced short. Here are a few examples

تَبَنَّى	ثَنَى	بَنَى
tabanna	*thana*	*bana*
to adopt	to fold, fold up	to build

‍ا and ء

ا (*'alif*) is one of the simplest letters of the alphabet. Its isolated form is simply a vertical stroke, written from top to bottom.

In its final position it is written as the same vertical stroke, but joined at the base to the preceding letter. Because of this connecting line — and this is very important — it is written from bottom to top instead of top to bottom.

Practise these to get the feel of the direction of the stroke.

The letter *'alif* is one of a number of *non-connecting* letters. This means that it is *never* connected to the letter that comes after it. Non-connecting letters therefore have *no initial or medial forms*. They can appear in only two ways: isolated or final, meaning connected to the preceding letter.

Reminder about pronunciation
The letter *'alif* represents the long vowel *aa*. Usually, this vowel sounds like a lengthened version of the *a* in *pat*. In some positions, however (we will explain this later), it sounds more like the *a* in *father*.

One of the most important functions of *'alif* is not as an independent sound but as the carrier, or 'bearer', of another letter: *hamza* (ء). Turn back to p. 29 and re-read what we said about *hamza* there. Later on we will discuss *hamza* in more detail. Here we will go through one of the most common uses of *hamza*: its combination with *'alif* at the beginning of a word.

One of the rules of the Arabic language is that *no word can begin with a vowel*. Many Arabic words may sound to the beginner as though they start with a vowel, but in fact they begin with a glottal stop: that little catch in the voice that is represented by *hamza*. When *hamza* appears at the start of a word, it is *always* written on *'alif*. The *'alif* in these cases *has no sound of its own*: it is simply acting as the carrier of *hamza*. If the vowel that follows the *hamza* is a short *a* or *u*, then the *hamza* and the vowel are written on top of the *'alif*; if the vowel is a short *i*, then both the *hamza* and the vowel are written below the *hamza*.

We therefore have

أ	أ	إ
'a	*'u*	*'i*

Finally, there is a special symbol, called *madda*, which is used to represent the sound of a *hamza* followed by a long vowel *aa* (in other words, *hamza* followed by *'alif*). The purpose of the *madda* is to avoid the ugly juxtaposition of two *'alifs*. This has already been explained in chapter 2, but here it is again:

آ represents the sound *'aa*.

Here are some practice words that illustrate the use of *'alif* and *hamza*.

أَنْتَ	أَنَا	آب	أَب
'anta	*'anaa*	*'aab*	*'ab*
you (masculine)	I	August	father

أَيَّات	أَنْتِ	بَنَات	أَيْنَ
'ayyaat	'anti	banaat	'ayna
verses of the Koran	you (feminine)	girls	where

تَابَ	بَاتَ	بَاب	بَابَا
taaba	baata	baab	baabaa
to repent	to spend the night	door	Pope

و

و (*waaw*) is another non-connecting letter. Remember that this means that it can be written only standing alone or connected to the preceding letter. It is never connected to the following letter, so there are no initial or medial forms.

Isolated, the loop sits on the line, and the tail extends below the line.

In the final position, it is written the same way, except for the little connecting line.

Reminder about pronunciation
The letter *waaw*, like *yaa'*, can represent either a consonant or a

long vowel or a diphthong. As a consonant, it has the sound of *w* in the word *wood*. As a long vowel, it has the sound of *oo* in *fool*. As a diphthong, it has the sound of *ow* in *how*. The principle by which you can tell what sound *waaw* has in any given word is exactly the same as for *yaa'*, so it might be a good idea to read that explanation again now.

Examples of the use of *waaw*:

أَوْثَان	أَوْ	وَثَبَ	وَ
'awthaan	*'aw*	*wathaba*	*wa*
idols	or	to jump	and

نَوَوِيّ	أُوبْرا	آوَى	تُوت
nawawiiy	*'uubraa*	*'aawa*	*tuut*
nuclear	opera	to harbour, shelter	mulberry

Recap of what we have learned so far

We have now covered all the vowels of written Arabic, three short

$$\bar{} \qquad \overset{\mathbf{o}}{} \qquad \overset{}{\diagup}$$

$$i \qquad\qquad u \qquad\qquad a$$

and three long

ﺐﻳﻲ ﻭﻭﻭ ﻭ ﻟﺍﺍ

51

We have also covered the two diphthongs

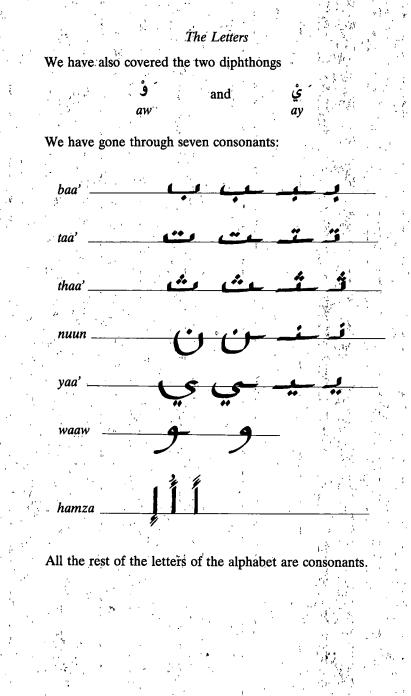

وْ

and

يْ

aw

ay

We have gone through seven consonants:

baa'

taa'

thaa'

nuun

yaa'

waaw

hamza

All the rest of the letters of the alphabet are consonants.

د   ذ

د (*daal*) and ذ (*dhaal*) have exactly the same shape, except that dhaal has a dot over the letter, where *daal* has none. These letters are both non-connecting, so they have no initial or medial forms.

Isolated

Final

Notice that the isolated and final forms have slightly different shapes. In the isolated form, the downstroke is a bit longer than the base stroke. Both forms sit squarely on the line: try not to let them sink below the line. The dot over the *dhaal* sits just above the letter.

Isolated

Final

Reminder about pronunciation
The *daal* is pronounced almost exactly as the English letter *d*.
The *dhaal* is like the *th* in *then*. Notice that Arabic has two.

different letters to represent the two distinct sound of *th*: as in *think* (*thaa'*) and as in *then* (*dhaal*).

Examples:

بَنْد	ذُبَاب	بَدو	دُنْيا
band	*dhubaab*	*baduu*	*dunyaa*
point of law	flies (insect)	bedouins	world

دِين	ذُنُوب	ذَابَ	أَدَب
diin	*dhunuub*	*dhaaba*	*'adab*
religion	sins	to melt	literature

نَبَذَ	آذان
nabadha	*'aadhaan*
to banish	ears

ر ز

Here we have two more non-connecting letters: no initial or medial forms, only isolated and final. The two letters form a pair, being identical except that *zaay* has a dot above where *raa'* has none.

Isolated

Final

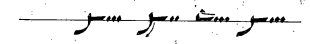

Isolated

Final

Notice that the basic shape begins just above the line and extends below the line. Also, be careful of the proportions: the top stroke is much shorter than the bottom one. The differences in these proportions and in the positioning on the line help to distinguish *raa'* and *zaay* on the one hand from *daal* and *dhaal* on the other.

Reminder about pronunciation
The letter *raa'* is similar to the English *r*, but is made by a flap of the tongue behind the teeth. The sound of *zaay* is almost exactly like the English *z*.

Examples:

دُود   بَرْد   رَبّ

duud   *bard*   *rabb*
worms   cold   lord

وَزِيْر
waziir
minister

زَبُوْن
zabuun
client

وَزْن
wazn
weight

دَرَّبَ
darraba
to train

رَتَّبَ
rattaba
to arrange

رَدَّ
radda
to give back

زَيْتُوْن
zaytuun
olives

تَزْوِيْر
tazwiir
forgery

زَوَّدَ
zawwada
to supply
provide

ش س

س (*siin*) and ش (*shiin*) are connecting letters. They therefore
have four forms each: isolated, initial, medial, and final. The
letters are identical except that *shiin* has three dots, where *siin*
has none.

Initial

Medial

The initial and medial versions of *siin* are very similar, the only difference being the little connector at the front of the medial form. Be careful not to make the peaks too high, and notice that the letters sit right on the line.

The final version has a tail that descends below the line and rises up above the line level with the peaks:

In isolation it looks the same, but without the connector:

The three dots of *shiin* are arranged in a triangle just like the three dots of *thaa'*. They are written above the little peaks, *not* above the tail.

Initial

Medial

Final

Isolated

Reminder about pronunciation:
The *siin* stands for the same sound as *s* in the word *sleep*. It *never* has a *z* sound as the English *s* sometimes does. The *shiin* has the same sound as the *sh* in *sheep*. Be careful not to confuse them.

Examples:

بَارِيس	بُسْتَان	سُورِيًّا
baariis	*bustaan*	*suuriiya*
Paris	orchard	Syria

بَشَر	شَرِبَ	دَرْس
bashar	*shariba*	*dars*
human being	to drink	lesson

سُودَان	وَشْوَشَ	نَتَشَ
suudaan	*washwasha*	*natasha*
Sudan	to whisper	to unplug

بَاشَا	شَبَاب	دُسْتُور
baashaa	*shabaab*	*dustuur*
pasha	youth (as noun)	constitution

شَاي	أُسْتَاذ
shaay	*'ustaadh*
tea	professor

ع غ

These two letters are fairly difficult, in both pronunciation and writing. They are both connectors, having four forms each, and differ only in one respect: *ghayn* has a dot over it, *ᶜayn* has none.

Isolated

Notice that the first part of *ᶜayn* looks very much like a *hamza*, only larger. It sits more or less on the line, while the bottom part of the letter sweeps below the line. The letter has to be made in two separate strokes, and be careful about the proportions.

The initial version of *ᶜayn* consists basically of the top part of the letter, the broad tail replaced by a connecting line to the following letter:

The medial version is a kind of altered form of the initial version. It is a flattened loop, resting just on the line. It has to be made in three strokes, with two changes of direction of the pen:

The final version begins just like the medial version, but then has a sweeping tail very much like the isolated version:

Making this letter in its various forms takes practice. It is the change of direction of the pen that makes it difficult, and it is essential to maintain the graceful proportions of the shape. Here are the various versions of *ghayn:*

Isolated

Initial

Medial

Final

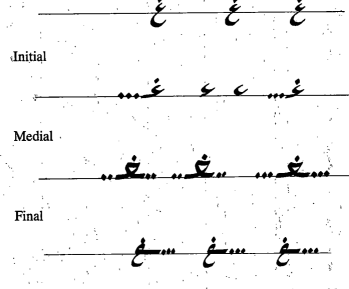

Look carefully at the following two sets as a further guide

Reminder about pronunciation
Look back at the section of chapter 2 explaining the pronunciation of these letters. Unfortunately, there is no way to make them any easier. It is simply a matter of practice and more practice.

Examples:

نَوْع	رَبِيع	يَعْبُد	عَرَبِيّ
naw^c	*rabii^c*	*ya^cbud*	*^carabiiy*
kind, type	spring	to worship	Arab

زَغْزَغَ	تَبْغ	بَغْداد	غَرْبِيّ
zaghzagha	*tabgh*	*baghdaad*	*gharbiiy*
to tickle	tobacco	Baghdad	western

م

م (*miim*) is another connector, with four forms. Basically, it consists of a flattened circle, with a descending tail that appears only in the final position. In some handwriting styles, and even in some typefaces, the circle is filled in, and looks like a large dot. The forms are:

Initial

Medial

Final

61

Isolated

To see the variation in forms, look at the following string of *miim* shapes:

If you look back at the table of ligatures on p. 35, you will see that there are various versions of integrating *miim* with other letters. The position of the basic shape is really quite flexible.

Reminder about pronunciation
The letter *miim* has the same sound as the English letter *m*.

Examples:

شَمْس	نَعَم	ثَمَن	مِنْ
shams	*naᶜam*	*thaman*	*min*
sun	yes	price	from

مُرَبَّع	نَوْم	ثُوم	ثُمَّ
murabbaᶜ	*nawm*	*thuum*	*thumma*
square	sleep (noun)	garlic	then

ل

ل (*laam*) is another connecting letter, with four forms.

Isolated

ل لٖ اٖ↓ ل

Notice that the stroke begins well above the line, descends below it, and then curls back up to meet the line. Be careful of the proportions: this letter is much taller than it is wide.

The final form is like the isolated form, but with a connector attaching it to the previous letter:

ل•• لٖ•• اٖ•• ل•• ل•••

Be careful not to make too thick a line as you double it by going first up and then down.

In an initial position, *laam* simply loses its tail

ل ••ل ••ل

In the medial position, it is the same as the initial version, but with two connectors

••ل•• ••ل•• ل•• ••ل••

Be careful not to confuse the initial or medial *laam* with *'alif*. Remember that *laam* is connected to the following letter, whereas *'alif* is not. Here is a string showing all the forms of *laam* connected to one another

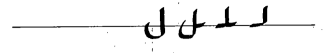

Reminder about pronunciation
The letter *laam* is pronounced like the English *l*, except that it is almost always a very pure, liquid sound, not muffled as the English *l* sometimes is. It sounds like the *l* in *light*, not like the *l* in *fool* or *feel*.

One special symbol that it is important to recognize is the combination of *laam* and *'alif*. When the sound *laa* occurs — an *l* followed by the long vowel *aa* — the *laam* and *'alif* are written together.

Isolated

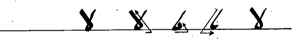

Final

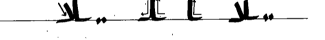

In the isolated form, *laam-'alif* gives the sound *laa*, which in Arabic is the word for 'no'.

Examples:

نَبِيل	بُلْبُل	لِسَان
nabiil	*bulbul*	*lisaan*
noble	nightingale	tongue

لَمَّا

lammaa
when

ثُلْث

thulth
two-thirds

رَسُول

rasuul
messenger

لَوْلَا

lawlaa
were it not
for

سَلَام

salaam
peace (used
as greeting)

لَازِم

laazim
necessary

Definite article

The definite article in Arabic — in other words, the word 'the' —
is

اَلْـ ... or ... اَلَـ ...

It is written attached to the word following it, which is why, in
most transliterations, it is represented as *al-*. Here are some
examples of words with and without the definite article:

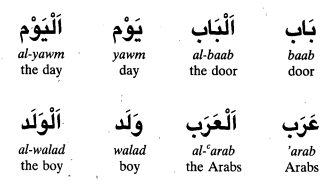

اَلْيَوْم

al-yawm
the day

يَوْم

yawm
day

اَلْبَاب

al-baab
the door

بَاب

baab
door

اَلْوَلَد

al-walad
the boy

وَلَد

walad
boy

اَلْعَرَب

al-ᶜarab
the Arabs

عَرَب

'arab
Arabs

When attaching the definite article to the word that follows it, we have to take account of the fact that the letters of the Arabic alphabet are divided into two categories, 'sun letters' and 'moon letters'. There are fourteen sun letters (named after the word *shams*, 'sun'). They are:

ت ث د ذ ر ز س ش ص ض ط ظ ل ن

As you will notice, most of them are either 'dentals' (made by touching the tongue to the teeth) or 'sibilants' (hissing sounds), which in Arabic are considered not to combine well with the sound *l*. The moon letters (named after the word *qamar*, 'moon') are all the other letters of the alphabet.

Now, when the definite article is connected to a word that begins with a sun letter, two things happen: the *sukuun* ('zero vowel') on the letter *laam* disappears, and a *shadda* (the doubling sign) is written above the sun letter. In pronunciation, the *laam* disappears and the sun letter is pronounced doubled. In effect, the *laam* is assimilated to the first letter of the word. Here are some examples:

<div dir="rtl">اَلرَّسُول</div>	<div dir="rtl">رَسُول</div>	<div dir="rtl">اَلدِّين</div>	<div dir="rtl">دِين</div>
ar-rasuul	*rasuul*	*ad-diin*	*diin*
the messenger	messenger	the religion	religion

<div dir="rtl">اَلنَّبِيّ</div>	<div dir="rtl">نَبِيّ</div>	<div dir="rtl">اَلشَّمْس</div>	<div dir="rtl">شَمْس</div>
an-nabiiy	*nabiiy*	*ash-shams*	*shams*
the prophet	prophet	the sun	sun

The *hamza* in the definite article is a *hamza* of a special type, called *hamzatu-l-waSl*, which means 'connecting *hamza*'. Strictly speaking, at the beginning of a sentence it should be written above the *'alif* like a normal *hamza*. In practice, however, it is usually not written, though it is pronounced in the normal way (as a glottal stop).

But if it comes in the middle of a phrase, the *hamzatu-l-waSl* is written above *'alif* as a kind of small loop above the *'alif*, but is not pronounced at all. It is elided, which simply means that it drops out. For example

بَابُ ٱلْبَيْتِ

baabu-l-bayt
the door of
the house

اَلْعَرَب وَ ٱلْغَرْب

'al-ᶜarab wa-l-gharb
the Arabs and
the West

اَلْوَلَد وَ ٱلرَّجُل

'al-walad wa-r-rajul
the boy and
the man

ك

ك (*kaaf*) is a connecting letter, with four forms.

Isolated

كـ اكـ اكبـ اكـ اك

Notice that the letter rests on the line, and be careful not to make the curl at the end too big. The wiggle in the lap of the letter looks very much like a *hamza*, but is simply an integral part of *kaaf*, like the dot over an *i* or *j* in English.

Final

The final form is essentially the same as the isolated, but with a connecting line.

Initial

Always do the top stroke *after* the first stroke of the body of the letter.

Medial

This form is like the initial form, but with a connector. Also, notice that the isolated and final forms are upright, while the initial and medial forms slope to the left.

Examples

كَلَام	سُكَّر	مَلِك
kalaam	*sukkar*	*malik*
speech, talk	sugar	king

مَلّاك	سُلُوك	إنْجِلِيز
mallaak	*suluuk*	*'injiliiz*
landowner	behaviour	English people

ج ح خ

These three letters have exactly the same shape, except that *jiim* has a dot below, *Haa'* has no dot at all, and *khaa'* has a dot above. They are connectors, with four forms.

Isolated

The top section of the letter stands above the line, while the tail extends well below.

Final

This is basically the same shape, but with a connector from the preceding letter.

The initial and medial forms essentially consist of the top of the letter, with the tail eliminated.

Initial

Medial

Note the position of the dot.

Haa' is exactly the same as *jiim*, but with no dot.

Finally, *khaa'* is the same, but with the dot above the letter. Note the position of the dot in the various forms.

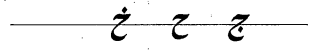

Reminder about pronunciation
Of these three letters, *jiim* is the easiest to pronounce. It is like the *s* in *pleasure* (the same as *j* in French). The letter *Haa'* is, strictly speaking, an unvoiced version of ‘*ayn* (see pp. 25-26 again for an explanation of this), and sounds like a very emphatic *h*. Finally, *khaa'* is the *ch* in the Scottish *loch*. Try to be careful not to make it too guttural, though it does come from the back of the mouth.

Examples

مَسِيْح	نَحْل	حُبّ
masiiH	*naHl*	*Hubb*
messiah, Christ	bee	love

مَجْنُون	جَدِيد	سِلاَح
majnuun	*jadiid*	*silaaH*
mad	new	weapon

خَمْر	أَعْوَج	ثَلِج
khamr	*'a‘waj*	*thalij*
wine	crooked	ice, snow

شُيُوخ شَيْخ بَخِيل

shuyuukh *shaykh* *bakhiil*
sheikhs sheikh greedy

خُبْز مُسْلِم مُحَمَّد

khubz *muslim* *muHammad*
bread Muslim Muhammad

ه

ه (*haa'*) is unusual in that there is hardly any resemblance between the various forms.

Isolated

ه (ۂ (ـھ ـه ـھ ـه

Notice that the shape is not quite round — it is more like an egg with a flattened bottom and slightly pointed top.

Initial

هـ هﮧ لهۂ لـ هـ

Although it looks very different, this form is actually similar to the isolated form, the middle stroke being a connector to the following letter.

Medial — here there are two types

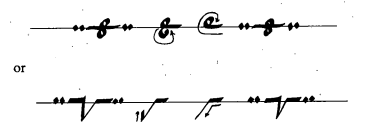

or

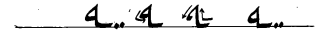

Both of these forms may be used in printed text in a book or newspaper. In handwriting, the second one is far more common. Be able to recognize both, but practice making the second one.

Final

Notice that the rounded part of this form stands slightly above the line, unlike the isolated form, which sits on the line.

Reminder about pronunciation
The letter *haa'* represents the same sound as the English letter *h*. There is therefore no difficulty pronouncing it, but notice that, unlike the English *h*, it can (and does) appear at the end of words. Make sure to pronounce it when this happens.

This is a good place to recall the letter *taa' marbuuTa*, which we mentioned earlier (see chapter 2). The *taa' márbuuTa* is basically just a letter *haa'* with two dots added over it (just like the two dots of the letter *taa'*). In general, the *taa' marbuuTa* is a sign that a word is grammatically feminine. It can occur *only* at the end of a word. When a word with *taa' marbuuTa* is pronounced in isolation, there is no *t* sound, and it is as if the word ended with a simple *haa'*. But when a word with *taa' marbuuTa* is immediately followed by another word (as in the last example below), it is pronounced as if it were a simple *taa'*. (Note carefully the transliteration below.) In other words, *taa' marbuuTa* is a kind of combination of *taa'* and *haa'*, and has the sound of the one or the other depending on the context.

Examples

نَهْر	هِيَ	هُوَ	إِنْتِبَاه
nahr	*hiya*	*huwa*	*'intibaah*
river	she	he	attention

مِرْوَحَة	مُسَاعَدَة	أَللَّه
mirwaHa	*musaaᶜadah*	*allah*
fan	help, aid	God

اَلْمَمْلَكَةُ ٱلْعَرَبِيَّةُ ٱلسَّعُودِيَّة

'al-mamlakatu-
l-ᶜarabiiyatu-
s-saᶜuudiiyah
the Kingdom of
Saudi Arabia

ض ص

ص (*Saad*) and ض (*Daad*) are identical in shape, except that the first has no dot, while the second has one dot above it.

Isolated

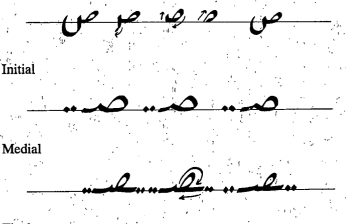

Initial

Medial

Final

Notice that in the isolated form, the first part of the letter sits on the line, while the tail drops below the line. The initial form is simply the isolated form with the tail missed out. The medial form is just the initial form with a connector added, and the final form is like the isolated form with an extra connector. One very important point: in *all* forms, do not miss out the little blip at the end of the letter, before the tail.

Notice that *Daad* is just the same as *Saad*, but with a dot. Also notice the position of the dot. Try not to make it too high above the letter.

74

Isolated

Initial

Medial

Final

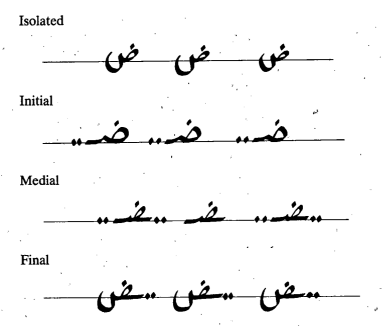

Reminder about pronunciation
The letter *Saad* is the emphatic version of the letter *siin*. The letter *Daad* is the emphatic version of the letter *daal*. Look back at p. 24 for an explanation of the pronunciation. Another point to note: when *'alif* comes after a *Saad* or *Daad*, or after the other emphatic consonants (*Taa'* and *DHaa'*: see pp. 76-78), it has the sound of *a* as in *father*. Try to remember the pairings:

د ـ ض   س ـ ص

Examples

إمْتِصَاص   مَغْص   بَصَل   صِنَاعَة

'imtiSaS	maghS	baSal	Sinaaᶜah
suction	colic	onion	industry

75

أَبْيَض	حَضَارَة	ضَخْم
'abyaD	*HaDaarah*	*Dakhm*
white	civilization, culture	huge

نَهَضَ	صَيَّاد	أَرْض
nahaDa	*Sayyaad*	*'arD*
to rise	hunter	land, earth

ظ   ظ   ط

ط (*Taa'*) and ظ (*DHaa'*) are relatively easy letters to write, because they have the same form in all positions, the only difference being the connecting strokes in the appropriate places. The only difference between the two letters themselves is that *DHaa'* is written with a dot above, where *Taa'* has none.

Isolated

ط   ظ   ظ   ط

Initial

طـ   طـ   طـ

Medial

ـطـ   ـطـ   ـطـ

76

Final

ظ ... ظ ... ظ ...

Notice that in all cases the loop is made first, then the downstroke is put on last. In writing words, it is usually easier to put on the downstroke after you have finished the entire word. Notice that the dot on *DHaa'* seems to nestle in the nook formed by the downstroke.

Isolated

ظ ظ ظ

Initial

... ظ ... ظ ... ظ

Medial

.. ظ .. ظ ... ظ ...

Final

ظ ... ظ ... ظ ...

Reminder about pronunciation
The letter *Taa'* is the emphatic version of the letter *taa'* (see p. 24 again). Strictly speaking, the letter *DHaa'* is the emphatic version of the letter *dhaal*. Many Arabs, however, pronounce *DHaa'* as an emphatic version of *zaay*, in which case it would be *Zaa'* instead of *DHaa'*. Either pronunciation is legitimate, so you can use whichever you find easier. Remember the pairings:

ت ـ ط · · ذ ـ ظ · ظ

Examples

نَفْط	مَطْبَخ	طِبّ
nafT oil	*maTbakh* kitchen	*Tibb* medicine
مَظْهَر	أَبو ظَبي	ضَرَطَ
maDHhar appearance	*'abu DHabi* Abu Dhabi	*DaraTa* to fart
طَبَعَ	مَحْظُوظ	غَليظ
Taba^ca to print	*maHDHuuDH* lucky	*ghaliiDH* boorish
ظُهْر	بَطَل	ضَابِط
DHuhr noon	*baTal* hero	*DaabiT* officer

ف ق

ف (*faa'*) and ق (*qaaf*) have shapes that are similar in certain respects. Both are basically loops with tails, but the contours of the loops and their positioning are different. In addition, *faa'* has one dot, whereas *qaaf* has two. Let's take *faa'* first.

Isolated

Notice that the loop sits on the line and that the tail is long and flat: it, too, sits on the line. The tip of the tail does not rise higher than the body of the letter.

Final

This is the same as the isolated form, but with a connector from the preceding letter.

The initial and medial forms simply drop the tail.

Initial

Medial

In the letter *qaaf* the loop is wider and, in the initial and isolated form, sits slightly above the line, while the tail in the isolated and final forms drops below the line (unlike *faa'*).

Initial

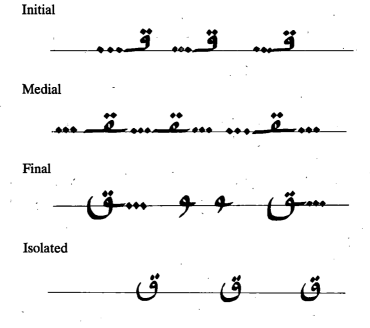

Medial

Final

Isolated

The tail of *qaaf* is shorter and rounder than the tail of *faa'*, and remember that *faa'* never goes below the line.

Reminder about pronunciation
The letter *faa'* is pronounced just like the English *f*. The *qaaf* is similar to the English *q*, but is made much further back in the throat (see chapter 2).

Examples

خَرِيف	تُفَّاح	فِلَسْطِينِي
khariif	*tuffaH*	*filasTiinii*
autumn	apples	Palestinian

خَرُوف	قَلْب	فَقِير
kharuuf	*qalb*	*faqiir*
sheep	heart	poor

صَدِيق	فُنْدُق	فَم
Sadiiq	*funduq*	*fam*
friend	hotel	mouth

إِفْرِيقِيَا	قُرْآن	لَفْظ
'ifriiqiyaa	*qur'aan*	*lafDH*
Africa	Koran	pronunciation

That completes our survey of the letters of the Arabic alphabet. We have now covered all the letters and symbols: everything you need to know to be able to read anything in Arabic. In the next section, we will give some examples of actual sentences from the Koran. Try to read them directly, using the transliteration only as a guide if you are stuck. All the required information has now been given. From here on, it is just a question of practice.

4 REFERENCE MATERIAL

HAMZA

In chapters 2 and 3 we explained that when the letter *hamza* occurs at the beginning of a word, it always 'rides' on an *'alif*. But we also mentioned that the glottal stop in Arabic, represented by *hamza*, is a full-fledged consonant that can occur anywhere in a word. When it appears in the middle or at the end of a word, *hamza* can 'ride' on any one of three letters: *'alif* (ﺍ), *waaw* (ﻭ), or *yaa'*, which is written without the two dots when it 'carries' *hamza* (ﻯ). Or, it can sit on the line independently.

Here are some examples of how *hamza* looks in the middle of a word.

سُؤَال   مَسْؤُول   رَأْس   كَأْس

قِرَاءَة   مُرُوءَة   قَائِم   سُئِلَ

Here are some examples of how it looks at the end of a word

لُؤْلُؤ   جَرُؤَ   قَرَأَ   بَدَأَ

سَمَاء   بَدْء   خَطِىءَ   نَاشِىء

Now, how can you determine which of the three letters — *'alif*, *waaw*, *yaa'* — will act as the 'carrier' of *hamza* in any given instance? As we mentioned before, the rules determining this are pretty complicated, and if the truth be told most foreigners learning Arabic (and indeed not a few Arabs) never really master them. The most important thing is to recognize *hamza* when you see it, and to build up an intuitive sense of which letter should 'carry' it.

For reference, however, here is a list of regulations that cover virtually every instance of the occurrence of *hamza*.

Initial position

When *hamza* appears at the start of a word, it is *always* written on *'alif*. If the vowel following *hamza* is *fatHa* (*a*) or *damma* (*u*), then *hamza* sits above *'alif*. If the vowel is *kasra* (*i*), then *hamza* is written below *'alif*. For example:

إِسْلَام   أُسْتَاذ   أَنْتَ

Medial Position

When it appears in the middle of a word, *hamza* is written over:

A. *'alif*
   a.) when the vowel of *hamza* is *fatHa* (*a*):

سَأَلَ

   b.) when the vowel of *hamza* is *sukuun* and the vowel preceding it is fatHa (*a*):

ثَأْر

B. *waaw*
   a.) when the vowel of *hamza* is *damma* (*u*):

بَؤُس

   b.) when the vowel of *hamza* is *sukuun* or *fatHa* (*a*) and the vowel preceding it is *damma* (*u*):

يُؤَلِّفُ   لُؤْم

C. *yaa'* (without the two dots)
   a.) when the vowel of *hamza* is *kasra* (*i*):

يَئِس   نَائِم   رَئِيس

b.) when the vowel preceding *hamza* is *kasra* (*i*):

بِئْر

c.) when *hamza* is preceded by the long vowel *ii* (*yaa'*), or is followed by the diphthong *ay* as in

جُزْئَيْن   رَدِيئَة   بِيئَة

D. without a carrier, sitting on the line
when the vowel of *hamza* is *fatHa* (*a*) and the preceding vowel is a long *aa* (*'alif*) or a long *uu* (*waaw*), as in

مُرُوءَة   قِرَاءَة

Final position

In the final position of word, *hamza* is written over

A. *'alif*
when the vowel preceding *hamza* is *fatHa* (*a*):

قَرَأ

B. *waaw*
when the vowel preceding *hamza* is *damma* (*u*):

دَنُؤَ

C. *yaa'* (without the two dots)
when the vowel preceding *hamza* is *kasra* (*i*):

خَطِىءَ   نَاشِىء

D. without a carrier, sitting on the line
a.) when *hamza* is preceded by *sukuun*:

بَدْء   شَيْء   عِبْء

b.) when *hamza* is preceded by a long vowel *aa* (*'alif*), *uu* (*waaw*), or *ii* (*yaa'*):

وُزَرَاء   وُضُوء   بَرِيء

A VERSE FROM THE KORAN

Finally, here is a sort of test, or more accurately, a challenge: a sample of classical Arabic prose. In fact, it is one of the most famous of all passages of classical Arabic: the Fatiha, or 'opening' (sometimes called the Exordium) of the Koran, the holy book of Islam. The Fatiha is one of the most commonly recited prayers of Islam, and may be regarded as a Muslim equivalent to the Lord's Prayer in Christianity. First we will give it to you in Arabic, fully vowelled. See if you can decipher it. After that, there is a line-by-line transliteration, followed by a line-by-line translation. It is worth going over it many times, as nearly all the letters of the alphabet appear in it. If you practise it enough, and find yourself able to read it, then you can be confident that you have truly mastered the Arabic alphabet.

سُورَةُ ٱلْفَاتِحَة

1   بِسْمِ ٱللّهِ ٱلرَّحْمَانِ ٱلرَّحِيمِ

2   أَلْحَمْدُ لِلّهِ رَبِّ ٱلْعَالَمِينِ

3   أَلرَّحْمَانِ ٱلرَّحِيمِ

4   مَالِكِ يَوْمِ ٱلدِّينِ

5   إِيَّاكَ نَعْبُدُ وَ إِيَّاكَ نَسْتَعِينُ

6   إِهْدِنَا ٱلصِّرَاطَ ٱلْمُسْتَقِيمَ

7   صِرَاطَ ٱلّذِينَ أَنْعَمْتَ عَلَيْهِمْ

8   غَيْرِ ٱلْمَغْضُوبِ عَلَيْهِمْ وَلَا ٱلضَّالِّينَ

Transliteration

suuratu-l-faatiHah

1. *bismi-l-laahi-r-raHmaani-r-raHiim.*

2. *al-Hamdu-lillahi rabbi-l-ᶜaalamiin.*

3. *ar-raHmaani-r-raHiim.*

4. *maaliki yawmi-d-diin.*

5. *'iyyaaka naᶜbudu wa 'iyyaaka nastaᶜiinu.*

6. *'ihdinaa-S-SiraaTa-l-mustaqiima.*

7. *SiraaTa-lladhiina 'anᶜamta ᶜalayhim.*

8. *ghayri-l-maghDuubi ᶜalayhim walaa-D-Daalliin.*

Reference Material

Translation

The Exordium

1. In the name of God (Allah), the compassionate, the merciful.

2. Praise be to God, Lord of the Worlds.

3. The compassionate, the merciful.

4. Master of Judgement Day.

5. You alone we worship, and to You alone we pray for help.

6. Guide us to the straight path.

7. The path of those whom You have favoured.

8. Not of those who have incurred Your wrath, nor of those who have gone astray.

(Adapted from the translation by N.J. Dawood: *The Koran*, Penguin Books, first published 1956, fourth revised edition 1976.)

A NOTE ON HANDWRITING

Although Arabic does not have the vast differences between printing and handwriting that English does, there are some variations in some of the letters when they are handwritten. Here are the most important ones.

The two dots of the letters *taa'*, *qaaf*, and *yaa'* are usually written as a dash.

ياقوت ياقوت يقتل يقتل

The three dots of the letters *thaa'* and *shiin* are usually written as a sort of inverted *v*, resembling a circumflex accent in French.

مثلث مثلث ثالث ثالث

شمس شمس مشمش مشمش

The blips of the letters *siin* and *shiin* are usually written as a flat line.

سمانو سمانو بطرس بطرس

مشمش مشمش سمانو سمانو

When the letter *yaa'* is connected to a final *nuun*, it is usually
written like this

شمين شمين أمين أمين

The letter *kaaf* in the initial position may be written like this

كان كان كل كل

In the final and isolated positions, the letters *nuun*, *shiin*, *Daad*,
and *qaaf* sometimes take on variant forms, as follows

أين أين إنسان إنسان

نتش نتش وشوش وشوش

رفض رفض عرض عرض

رفيق رفيق فندق فندق

THE ALPHABET

Table Showing All Forms

Name of Letter	Standing alone	Final	Medial	Initial
'alif	ا	ـا		
baa'	ب	ـب	ـبـ	بـ
taa'	ت	ـت	ـتـ	تـ
thaa'	ث	ـث	ـثـ	ثـ
jiim	ج	ـج	ـجـ	جـ
Haa'	ح	ـح	ـحـ	حـ
khaa'	خ	ـخ	ـخـ	خـ
daal	د	ـد		
dhaal	ذ	ـذ		
raa'	ر	ـر		
zaay	ز	ـز		
siin	س	ـس	ـسـ	سـ
shiin	ش	ـش	ـشـ	شـ
Saad	ص	ـص	ـصـ	صـ
Daad	ض	ـض	ـضـ	ضـ
Taa'	ط	ـط	ـطـ	ط

Dhaa'	ظ	ـظ	ـظـ	ظ
ʿayn	ع	ـع	ـعـ	عـ
ghayn	غ	ـغ	ـغـ	غـ
faa'	ف	ـف	ـفـ	فـ
qaaf	ق	ـق	ـقـ	قـ
kaaf	ك	ـك	ـكـ	كـ
laam	ل	ـل	ـلـ	لـ
miim	م	ـم	ـمـ	مـ
niuun	ن	ـن	ـنـ	نـ
haa'	ه	ـه	ـهـ	هـ
waaw	و	ـو		
yaa'	ي	ـي	ـيـ	يـ

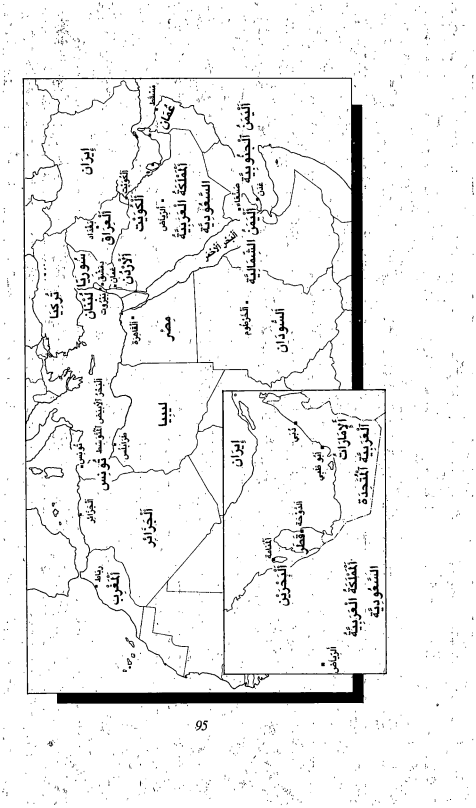